Be more Buffy

A guide to slaying every day

Be more
Buffy

A guide to slaying every day

ALEX CLARKE-GROOM

ILLUSTRATIONS BY YOUNGEARLGREY

Smith
Street
Books

PREPARE TO SLAY

When Buffy arrived in our lives in the mid-1990s, it was like a blast of fresh Californian air. It was an age defined by the shriek of dial-up internet, beeping pagers and un-ironic velvet hats. The idea of a badass super hero called Buffy, who happened to be both a cheerleader and the world's savior, was fresher than the Prince of Bel-Air, and millions were glued to her adventures.

While the show ended 17 years ago – pause for sharp intake of breath – television and streaming repeats and syndication mean millions more have fallen in love with Sunnydale's resident Slayer.

Buffy and the Scoobies are such an awesome group of characters that we never get bored of spending time with them. Depending on your mood, there's a Buffy episode to suit it. Want to laugh? Hello, Anya! Want to have a little weep? Bring on the Buffy and Angel episodes. Want to have a sing-a-long? There's even an episode for that!

One of the reasons that Buffy's such an incredible role model is that she's both ordinary and extraordinary at the same time. There's so much we can learn from her story, her battles and, importantly, her fails. Sometimes this modern, crazy world feels like the Hellmouth *did* actually open in 2003, so let's look for some guidance for our own lives from the ultimate hero, Buffy the Vampire Slayer.

Be more Buffy!

It's not an unreasonable assumption that a reader of a book called *Be More Buffy* might want to emulate the Great One herself but, you know, people are weird. So just in case you need a reminder of why we should all aspire to be more like the Buffster, here goes.

The great heroes have many qualities: incredible strength, stamina, grace, charm, kindness, humility and bravery.

And when we think of Buffy's main qualities? Yes, yes, yes, yes, yes, yes and HELL YES!

A pint-sized warrior for good, Buffy goes through all the crap things we do – high school, college, bad jobs, awful breakups, grief and loss – and deals with them the same way we do ... sometimes with stunning nobility, and other times crying on the couch eating Cheetos with a friend. We can identify. Yes she can drop-kick a marine across a room, but she also drops food down herself, breaks things, gets drunk, and sleeps with unsuitable people. Just like us.

Carrying the weight of the world on her shoulders, Buffy literally dies to save us, but does she see herself as a messiah who's here to save us all? Nope. She remains humble and hopeful for a world in which she can try and live a normal life, shouldering an unbelievable burden, which occasionally causes her to stumble, but never to fall.

Best Traits

Strong in every sense, brave, kind, loyal, wise-cracking, self-sacrificing ... oh, and she's the Chosen One – the list is endless. The right answer to any problem can often be found by asking "What would Buffy do" and, if we all did, the world would be a better place ... and we'd all have nicer hair too. Shout it out loud – I Want to Be More Buffy!

> " The hardest thing in this world is to live in it. Be brave. Live. "

"i AM THE THE PLAN."

DEALiNG NEW START WITH A

Buffy Summers arrived in the demon-ridden town of Sunnydale, California, with butterflies in her stomach. These nerves were pretty unsurprising, since, in a short period of time she'd been kicked out of her old school for accidentally burning down the gym while battling demons, her parents had split up, she'd had to leave her friends behind, had to move house and even city, and lost her first Watcher – all this before the ashes of Hemery High's gymnasium were cold.

Luckily most of us don't get saddled with a mystical destiny that ultimately causes our lives to be turned upside down. That isn't to say we don't sometimes have to say goodbye to all that's familiar, pack up our bags and start again somewhere else, where everything is strange and new. At some point we're all going to feel like that scared 16-year-old girl – although probably without a burgundy pleather mini-skirt and structured bangs.

New starts are hard but that doesn't mean they have to be awful. Despite Buffy's grades being described as "dismal," a dead boy showing up in a locker on day one, and receiving her first blast of shade from Cordelia, Buffy gets through it. What helps Buffy through those early days in Sunnydale isn't her mystical powers, but belief in herself, a positive attitude and an openness to meeting new people.

The takeaway

We all know that scary feeling of walking into a new classroom, college dorm or office, not knowing a soul. But, like Buffy, we just need to put our best heeled boot forward, trust in ourselves and realize that things won't feel strange for too long. You never know, maybe we'll bump into a tall, dark brooding immortal behind the garbage cans of our new local nightclub?

SLAYER SURVIVAL GUIDE

SURVIVING A WORK APOCALYPSE

So you've missed your deadlines, your boss's nostrils are flaring at you over your cubicle wall and you can't for the life of you think what that Post-It Note marked "Very important, do not forget!!!!" was ACTUALLY for. It may not be raining fire and demons outside but it's starting to feel like the End is very much Nigh.

In times like this it's worth thinking about what Buffy would do and prepare the following:

1. **Holy water and communion wafers:** While probably not needed for the same reason Buffy would have them, in a crisis you can use these to sustain you during an all-nighter at the office. Plus on the very, very unlikely chance that you're overrun by the Undead, you will have a weapon you can use ... Bonus!

2. **A book of spells:** While Buffy would likely outsource the magic to Willow, the ability to find a lost object or even to delete that knee-jerk email from someone's inbox, could come very much in handy. Yes, it's sort of cheating but if it works, who cares?

3. **A crucifix:** Again, who knows if this would work against an angry client, but you can always use it to pray to the Powers That Be for a miracle. Buffy's experienced them before, so maybe you'll get lucky too!

Affirmations

Stand in front of a mirror*
and repeat three times slowly:

1. I am strong and confident and
I will not let anyone put me down.

2. There is no ceiling for me.
I can change the world. A lot.

3. I am loved by the family I was born with
and the family I have chosen.

*If you don't have a reflection you have problems outside the scope of this book!

Life Lesson

THE iMPORTANCE of HAViNG FUN

If there was ever someone who probably shouldn't have gotten out of bed on her birthday, it's Buffy. At her 17th her boyfriend turned evil, her 18th involved being walled up with a psycho vampire, her 19th saw her Watcher, Giles, turned into a demon and on her 20th she had a showdown with The Beast, Glory!

In comparison, a few late cards and some no-shows from people who inexplicably develop bird flu on the day of your party should seem like nothing! As with all things the Buffmeister went through, despite tragedy, assault and Cordelia's dip, she never gave up hope of having a bash where no-one died

You can slay vampires and have a social life, but it's tricky. However, when you have a job as onerous as the Slayer's, you need to find some time to kick back, vogue up and have a kiki. Even if you're not ramming pieces of wood through vampires' chests every night, we all still need to enjoy a good party once in a while.

So what do you need for the perfect Buffy-style party (minus the inevitable world-ending disaster)?:

1. **Good friends:** These are essential. They are food for the soul.

2. **Snacks:** Both heathy AND deep-fried.

3. **Drinks:** While you don't need alcohol, you do need imagination. Make 'em interesting!

4. **Tunes:** While Oz's band the Dingoes would be the natural first choice, anything to create the perfect atmosphere is fine.

Life Lesson
LOVERS WITH A PAST

Falling in love can be simultaneously the greatest and scariest experience of all time. Most people wouldn't classify Angel and Buffy's relationship as normal, and they certainly had their problems ... even aside from his thirst for blood. Angel was a man with a past – 270 years of it in fact – and a relationship history filled with the bad, the mad and the frankly demented.

We can all relate to good-looking people driving us crazy although, in the case of Angel, he did literally drive Drusilla crazy. The epitome of late-90s hotness, Angel's tortured pouting had many hearts pulsating and begging to be staked long before the sulky *Twilight* Cullens were even conceived. However, Angel's exes kept turning up in his unlife – first Darla and then Drusilla – causing chaos. Here's how Buffy dealt with it:

1. **ACCEPTANCE:** She didn't like the fact that Angel made most bad boys look like poodles, but also accepted that his past was his past. If she had him in her life she had to accept his whole life's story.

2. **OPENNESS:** Buffy knew that Angel loved her and could see the proof of it nightly. As such, she allowed her heart to intertwine with his and didn't hold his previous life against him. She loved him for how he treated her, not who he used to be.

3. **WISDOM:** Despite the many terrible things that happened to them both, Buffy never stopped loving Angel. That isn't to say, though, that when his behavior changed she blindly went along with it. She saw it for what it was and let go ... probably one of the hardest battles she ever faced.

The takeaway

Falling in love is something many of us will experience at least once. Just remember that, while everyone has a past, you should judge your relationship on the here and now.

FIGHTING THE PATRIARCHY

> **"In every generation there is a Chosen one.
> She alone will stand against the vampires, the demons,
> and the forces of darkness. She is the Slayer."**

These words greeted us in the early days when we were still getting our heads around the Buffyverse. However, they're not entirely accurate as Buffy was never actually alone. From the earliest days she had her trusty Watcher, Giles, who trained and nurtured her abilities like a bespectacled, tea-drinking fairy godfather.

What eventually became clear was that Giles was the kind face of an ancient organisation called the Watchers Council, the epitome of Male, Pale and Stale. The other members of the Council saw Buffy as a mere tool, a weapon for them to wield in their battle against evil. Even a badass like Buffy took this BS for about two years before coming to an important realization – that the Council needed her way more than she needed them. Without her, they were nothing.

It's telling that a woman as smart, mature and brave as Buffy still took a while (and terrible circumstances – casual indifference to her undead lover's death from poison) to see the system for what it is – a group of men who used women to fight their battles and to boost their egos.

The takeaway

Even today, much of the world is controlled by the hands of a few powerful men and breaking through the glass ceilings that have been set can feel impossible. Two things helped Buffy that we can all learn from:

1. A refusal to accept that a group of men could and should set her future.

2. Belief in her own ability and judgment about how best to change her world.

If you have an equivalent of the Watchers Council in your life, tell them to close up shop as you're not working for them anymore. Your path is yours to choose.

Be more Xander!

In a world where everyone was either super strong, incredibly fast, had magical powers or immortality, all Xander had was a heart as deep as the ocean ... and some great jokes. It's frankly a miracle he's still alive considering the number of omnipotent evil beings he faced (which seem to be perpetually on 2-4-1 in the "Hell" aisle of Sunnydale market).

While he was relegated to the lovable idiot camp in the early days, he grew to become an attractive, confident man – who could rock a pair of red Speedos! He made mistakes – sleeping with Faith, cheating on Cordelia, dumping Anya – that, on paper, make him look like ... well ... an asshole. But the mistakes showed him to be human and he always atoned for what he did. Was he petty, jealous, fragile? Yes, but more importantly, he was kind and fiercely protective of his friends. He was human, with all the flaws that humans have.

Xander is in many ways the true hero in *Buffy*, especially to us mere mortals who don't have the strength to beat a demon to death. We learn that even if you are considered useless – a "zeppo" – you can still be brave. If you don't have a razor-sharp mind and a 4-point GPA you can still think of smart solutions.

Best Traits
Loyal to his friends, brave, a great sense of humor in the face of danger, emotional intelligence, kindness.

At some point we've all been the person who felt like the object of ridicule but, like Xander, our past doesn't have to define our future. His parents may not have loved him, he may have been the butt of everyone's jokes at high school, he made money stripping in a roadside bar, selling Boost bars and caught magical syphilis, but he kept going and growing until he stood by the Slayer's side and saved the world.

> **I don't handle rejection well. Funny considering how much practice I've had, huh?**

What would Buffy do?

GIRL BOSS

The World of Work

Buffy and the gang had a, shall we say, "mixed" experience of the world of work. While Anya discovered a deep love of retail, Xander drifted through a series of deeply depressing roles before finding his true calling in construction.

Buffy's only real experience was the awful Doublemeat Palace. And Willow? Willow never seemed to do a day's work, but when you can manipulate the elemental forces of nature, doing spreadsheets and dealing with Linda in accounts probably feels unnecessary.

Most of us, however, do have to get up every day for the old 9-to-5 and, while there are some perks to being at work (financial independence and free wi-fi anyone?), there are an awful lot of downsides, from psycho co-workers who steal credit for your work, to gross communal kitchens that even a chaos demon would be repulsed by – the list is endless.

So what would Buffy do about the horrors of the modern workplace?

Being undermined by a crazy boss: Most of us have had a bad boss or supervisor and, while savagely staking them in the heart might feel tempting, it's probably not the best solution. Buffy was forever being told she was nothing by the demonic forces set against her, but she always realized that it wasn't about her. Only by trying to make her feel small could these people make themselves feel tall. You are the only person responsible for your success, so don't let someone else take it away.

Team-bonding away days: A day spent making wicker baskets or playing paintball with your team can feel like a torture devised by the First Evil itself. Buffy would probably beg Willow to fast-forward time but, when that failed, she'd grit her teeth, put a smile on her face and pun her way through the day.

Sleazy dudes at the office party: This is one depressing constant that never seems to change. Buffy would be polite and sassy but firm. And if they didn't take the hint, she'd drop-kick them out the window – #getgone.

WHEN SEX CHANGES THINGS

One of the abiding characteristics of Buffy was that despite being the Chosen One she was decidedly unlucky in the bedroom department. Despite trying her best to seek out partners who would respect her, more often than not, once she got into bed with them (or memorably, in Spike's case, a collapsed basement) things tended to go seriously awry.

The most devastating time was when she lost her virginity to Angel on her sweet 17th, a day she's unlikely to treasure the memory of. Although to be fair to the Buffmeister, checking that your potential lover isn't the subject of a curse isn't top of the list of things most of us would check before bedding down with a new partner. We might ask:

Do they have fresh breath? Check!

Are we using protection? Absolutely!

Will he lose his soul when he climaxes? ... Not so much.

The takeaway

We've all been in those relationships where everything is heady and dreamy in the dateville stage, but you take it to the next level and then, boom! They never call again. One day you're a deity and the next you're nobody. We end up driving ourselves mad trying to work out why? What did I do wrong? Did I say something weird? On the other hand, *they* might never stop calling, and *you're* the one who needs space. Would this make Buffy fall in a heap of dust? No way!

You have to follow your heart and your instincts, but sometimes sex can change a relationship in a way you never knew how. At times it's magical and other times it's mercifully brief. The most important things are   that you look after yourself physically and mentally, respect each other, act with both of your best interests in mind and, most importantly, enjoy it!

DEALING WITH IMPOSSIBLE ODDS

At some point in our lives we'll come across a force that seems unstoppable, an authority that we feel powerless to prevent from running us over. These obstacles can go by many names but, in Buffy's life, it had a very specific one.

Mayor Richard Wilkins III was arguably Buffy's most monstrous opponent as, ironically, he wasn't a monster at all. He was a human with a relentless thirst for power and control, which drove him to seek mystical ways to become, ultimately, an enormous snake demon (a plan that always seemed impractical – is immortality really worth it if you don't have ARMS?).

The biggest issue Buffy faced was that in the run-up to the ascension, the Mayor was invulnerable, so this wasn't going to be a problem that Mr. Pointy, her trusty stake, could solve. Things got pretty desperate for a while but, once they realized they could destroy the Mayor AFTER he became a demon, a window for victory opened. Buffy rallies the whole graduating class for a plan so audacious, brave and ingenious that, when we see the Mayor slither into an explosives-laden library, our collective jaws hit the floor. This was Buffy at her most brilliant.

The Mayor was the ultimate power in town but, when we look at this scenario, we can see that "Dick" could be anyone in our life: the government, a boss or a teacher.

The takeaway

The whole experience has lessons for us all:

1. **Be open to a new approach:** When dealing with an impossible opponent sometimes only an impossible plan will do.

2. ***We* is stronger than *me*:** Even the Slayer needs allies, so marshall the troops if you want to win.

3. **If it's worth it, don't be afraid to blow everything up.**[*]

[*]This is a metaphor – please don't blow anything up!

Be more Giles!

Rupert Giles, Watcher, librarian, ex-70s wild child, mod rocker – truly a man for all seasons. When he first meets Buffy he is so British he practically bleeds English Breakfast tea, but their relationship relaxes and grows and, ultimately, he becomes her de facto father ... Buffy's biological one having less presence than the Invisible Man. We come to see that Giles loves Buffy in the way only a true father can.

Giles' steely intellect and noble bravery come into play over and over again. His first instinct is always to protect the Scoobies – yes, often from physical danger, but also crucially in other ways too. When he feels that his presence is holding Buffy back from taking control of her own life, he heads back to England. It's a heartbreaking decision for everyone, but 100 percent the right thing to do at the time.

This is the key lesson we can learn from Giles – that sometimes you have to do what feels wrong in order to do what's right. So, yes, he leaves at one point, but when Willow goes off the rails he is back to save her – and the world – from annihilation by magic. What a champ.

Best Traits

Kindness, genius-level intelligence, nobility, compassion, courage, a great leader, nurturing.

> **"** *I had very definite plans about my future. I was going to be a fighter pilot. Or possibly a grocer. Well, uh … My father gave me a very tiresome speech about, uh, responsibility and sacrifice.* **"**

Life Lesson

BEING A MENTOR

Looking after yourself is hard enough sometimes, but when Buffy opened the door to dozens of potential slayers, all seeking asylum after the Watchers Council was blown up by the First Evil, she must have thought "Crapbag – what do I do now?"

Having one hormonal disaster-magnet sibling was enough, but a whole house of teenage girls (with only one bathroom) must have felt like the beginning of the Apocalypse. Which it actually was, ironically.

Despite this, Buffy rose to the occasion, opening her house to a myriad of different girls from around the world who all needed someone – anyone – to save them. The responsibility of being a mentor and leader is one that we'll all come across in some aspect in our lives. Whether it's for our friends at school or college, our teammates in a sports situation, or as a parent, learning how to shape and nurture others is a key skill. Buffy turned a rag-tag team of girls into the ultimate weapon against evil. Here's what you can learn:

1. **Listen:** It's easy to think that mentoring is mostly about telling others what to do. The reality is that really listening to, and understanding, what is happening in the lives of your charges is the most crucial thing to being a good mentor.

2. **Lead by example:** If you're going to be the leading light in someone's life, then *you* have to be the person you want *them* to be.

3. **Respect other people's individuality:** Mentoring involves shaping and guiding a person, not creating a carbon copy of yourself. Show them the end destination but let them choose their own path.

What would Buffy do?

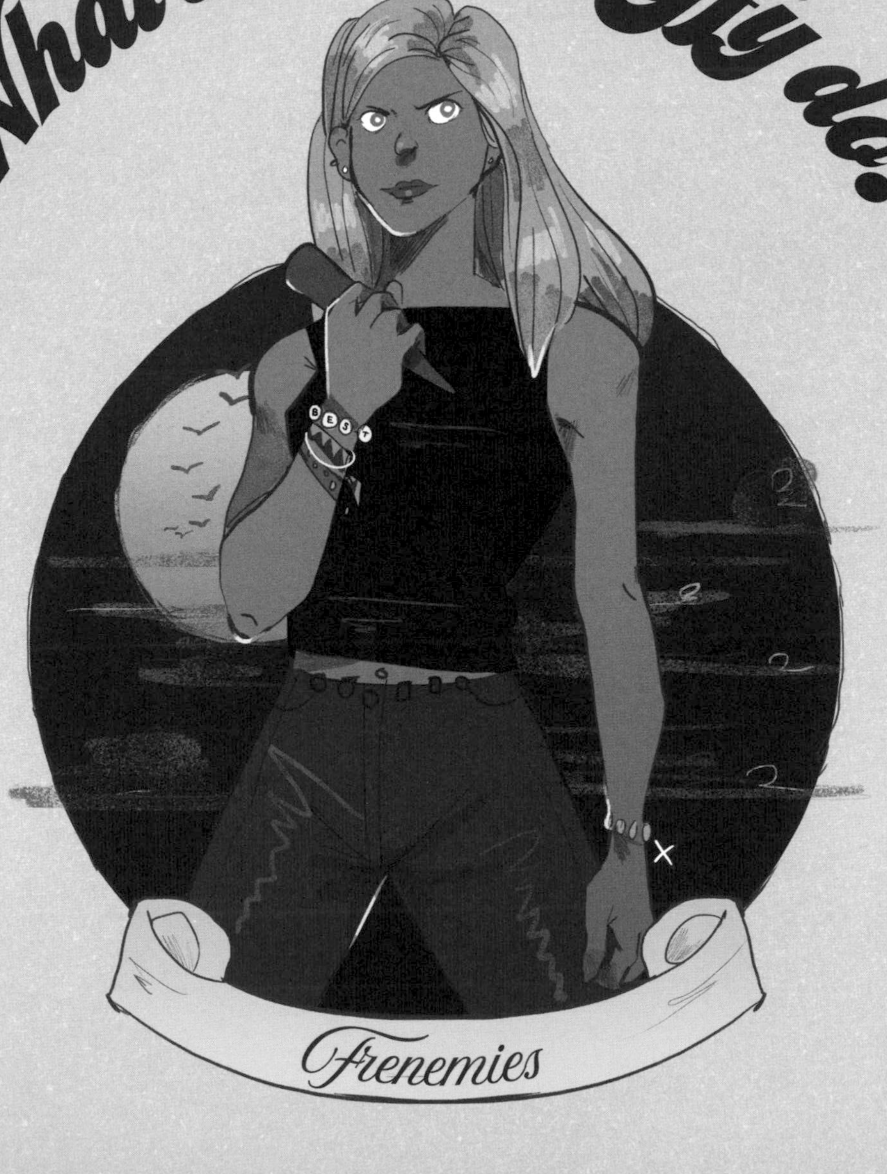

Ah the Scooby Gang, the best group of friends a Slayer could have. They were there for Buffy when she needed them, whether it was support for a bad breakup – high five, Willow – or detailed knowledge of how to break into the armory at the local military base – take a bow, Xander.

In this regard Buffy was blessed, but the Duchess of Buffonia also had her fair share of tricky friendships to manage, Cordelia being number 1. However, let's not forget Cordelia's brain-dead sidekick Harmony, and Faith "five by five" Lehane. When it came to these three, superpowers weren't much use – assaulting fellow high-school students wasn't really in the spirit of being the Chosen One. And Faith, well, Faith was basically CRAY CRAY.

So how would Buffy have dealt with that "friend" who "loves us" but we all know has a special chapter devoted to us in their Burn Book?

† **Accept you might not win:** Now this is hard for those of us used to slaying everything, but sometimes you need to let these type of people come out on top. Competing with them only makes them worse. Swallow your need to be number 1.

† **Question why you care so much:** Do you really care what these people think? Why? Maybe your desire to seek their approval is what gives them power over you?

† **Kill them … with kindness:** Nothing is more likely to annoy these people more than for you to respond to their shady remarks with a smile and thank you.

Buffy eventually reached an accord with Cordelia and Faith. While you would never say they were friends, they found a way to co-exist. As for Harmony, well she died, came back as a vampire, dated Spike and ended up as Angel's assistant, so it's probably fair to say Buffy had the last laugh!

" Strong is fighting! It's hard, and it's painful, and it's every day. It's what we have to do. And we can do it together. "

Be more
Willow!

Every hero needs a sidekick and, in Willow, Buffy has the best possible slay buddy. With brains bigger than Cordelia's ego, Willow provides a lot of the smart thinking that helps the Scoobies' plans to succeed. Once she begins practicing magic she becomes even more essential – her abilities proving to be the decisive factor in several key battles.

Yes things went a little awry towards the end and, yes, almost burning the world to ash doesn't scream "role-model," but actually we can learn so much from Ms. Rosenberg.

* Despite being picked on viciously by bullies, she doesn't let it make her bitter.

* Willow celebrates her love of knowledge and learning and never holds back from passing it on.

* Compassion is a magic in its own right.

* Bravery comes in many forms. Sometimes it's confronting our enemies, other times it's standing up and being proud of who you are.

Best Traits
Geeky in a great way, modest, intelligent, a powerful witch, super loyal, brave.

All the gang changed as they grew, but none more so than Willow. From a shy dorky girl in love with Xander, she becomes the most powerful witch in the world, forever altering the scales in the battle between good and evil – which is pretty nifty when you think about it!

"I'm not strong.
I'm not an
Amazon.
I'm just me."

DEALING WITH RIVALS

One of the great jokes of the Buffyverse is that the Chosen One is actually a Chosen Two! Due to a combination of Buffy's unfortunate death at the hands of the Master and Xander's CPR skills, a second Slayer is called. Fast-forward through a whole heap of conflama and you have the arrival in town of Buffy's ultimate rival – Faith.

The dark yin to Buffy's cheerleading yang, Faith was a leather-panted badass with a penchant for a purple lip. Initially she encouraged Buffy to rebel against the confines of her vocation and they became, for a while, best buds. Sadly it went rapidly downhill with Faith becoming a murderous psychopath in service to the Mayor – which is pretty hard to get beyond.

The takeaway

Having a rival can be tough and, at some point in our lives, we'll all have someone who tries to compete with us. Now healthy rivalry is a good thing, but it's easy to let it spiral out of control and end up in a pointless battle of who's better than who. What can we learn from the Buffinator?

1. **Question your actions:** Are you doing something because it's right, or because you want to win?

2. **Avoid collateral damage:** In our desire to win we can forget our usual values and others can get hurt.

3. **Try and see the person behind the rival:** Put aside your rivalry for a second and see if you can work out what makes your competitor tick. Maybe there's been a misunderstanding somewhere down the line, and they think you are the competitor.

SLAYER SURVIVAL GUIDE

SURVIVING A CRISIS IN YOUR PERSONAL LIFE

Disaster has struck, your love life is an endless nuclear winter and you're pretty sure the cat is only with you in case you drop dead, thereby becoming a handy food source. Things are BAD. Buffy would feel your pain as she could barely walk down the street without someone trying to bite/stab/beat/sting/peel/curse her. And, as for her love life, from the top: Undead, Creep, Secret Soldier, Dracula and Undead Asshole. She knew what it was like to have a crappy hand served to you. Did she let it bring her down, though? No stinking way!

Here's what you need to get through a life meltdown:

1. **Snacks:** Do not attempt to survive a crisis armed only with hummus. You need cookies, donuts and a vat of ice cream.

2. **Friends:** Get your Scooby Gang round asap, veg out on the couch and watch a movie. Do not try and be brave on your own.

3. **Perspective:** Very few things are as bad as they seem. The sun will always rise, and everything gets better with time. Give yourself the space to just relax and breathe.

4. **Go out there and do something for someone else:** When you stop focussing so much on your own problems you might find they don't weigh you down so much. It's a good feeling to help someone else with needs greater than your own.

Affirmations

Fighting for yourself is important, but fighting for others is what makes a true hero. Repeat the following to ensure that you're always ready to fight on someone's behalf:

1. By saving others I save myself.

2. A strong person stands up for themselves, a stronger person stands up for others.

3. If I don't help, who will?

HOW BUFFY ARE YOU?

Sometimes we all need a checkpoint, a little test to see how we're doing on whatever task we've focussed on. Answer thedr questions to see whether you're practically the next-in-line to be the Chosen One, or if you need to work on your slayage skills more.

Your bae is moody and secretive. They occasionally vanish in the middle of your dates and seem to be anguished all the time. Do you:

a) Accept it as part of them and never mention it.

b) Confront them about it – this is no way to treat me!

c) Observe them while doing a handstand on old piping in an alleyway.

d) Stalk them on social media while constructing elaborate theories.

You have a friend who is actually a real ass. You put up with their negativity all the time and never get anything back. What do you do?

a) Whine about them to your other friends? Why do they have to be such a b.i.t.c.h.?

b) Spill the tea about them publicly, then cancel them.

c) Rise above it as you recognize you have something more important to focus on.

d) Whisper shady things about them in return. Two can play at that game!

You're struggling at work. The hours are crazy, your boss is clearly an ex-vengeance demon and the pay is terrible. So you:

a) Tell everyone on social media how much your life sucks to get some sympathy.

b) Quit your job in an angry tirade, and tell them to BITE ME!

c) Keep plugging away. You need the money and at least you have a job.

d) Play petty pranks against your company to get some revenge.

A new colleague joins your team and they're perfect – super smart, confident, makes friends easily, yada yada yada. How do you feel about them?

a) Feel incredibly intimidated but hide it by appearing disinterested.

b) CRUSH them. Go out of your way to show them that you're number 1 round here.

c) Take some time to get to know them and find out what you can learn.

d) Bitch about them furiously to anyone who comes anywhere near you.

Your friend's partner always belittles them in public and often reduces them to tears. Your friend used to be the life and soul, but now seems like they've had the life drained out of them. What do you do?

a) Ignore it most of the time and, when you can't, change the subject asap.

b) Find the chunkiest ring you own before giving their partner the biggest telenovela slap you can muster.

c) Help your friend to build up their courage to confront and, if necessary, leave that douchebag.

d) Roll your eyes behind their back – stop being such a wuss!

Someone confesses to you that they have a major crush on you but, to be frank, the mere thought of it gives you the wiggins. Do you:

a) Avoid. Avoid. Avoid. Can't hunt what you can't find!

b) Blurt out that you'd rather French kiss the Master.

c) Let them down gently but, if they try anything, you'd stake that bubble fast.

d) Laugh in their face. Would Cordelia date Jonathan Levinson? I don't think so!

Your sibling is being a major pain. They literally can't do anything without messing it up. What do you say to them?

a) For god's sake, you are so annoying! Leave me alone!

b) God I wish you'd turn back into a ball of green energy!

c) Stay here, stay safe. I need to protect you.

d) Hey, is that Glory? I have to tell you about my sibling, Dawn.

You have a secret vocation, a job no-one else in the world can do. How do you feel about it?

a) Terrified. Why does this have to be all my responsibility?

b) Yeehaw! Awesome! I get to do anything I want, when I want. I'm like a god!

c) Jeepers. This is a huge responsibility, but I have to get it right for everyone's sake.

d) Oh greeeeat. Like I literaly have no time for this.

ANSWERS

Mostly As

You need to stand up for yourself more! Yes, sometimes things in life suck (as well as vampires!), but sitting and watching them happen is not going to solve them. Buffy survived multiple dramas in her life by hitting her problems head on. Doing something is ALWAYS better than doing nothing.

Mostly Bs

Woah! Down girl! Someone's been channeling a fair bit of their inner Faith! Yes, the world can be shitty sometimes, but fighting fire with fire all the time means sometimes you're going to get burned. Buffy knew when to go in hard, sure, but she also knew when she was acting a little overly hasty and needed to stop, reflect and think of a plan.

Mostly Cs

Psssst. Buffy, over here! Wow. You really could be the Chosen One! You're hardworking, noble and pretty spry. You don't need any advice ... just keep on being you!

Mostly Ds

Yikes. You need to sit and have a bit of a think about your behavior. Sure, you may be dealing with a lot, but this is not the approach Buffy would take. When life wrongs you, don't try and wrong it back. Think what our hero the Buffster would do, and follow her path.

Be more Cordelia!

Cordelia manifests in her early days as a straight-up, 24-carat bitch, a stereotypical mean girl who terrorizes the Scoobies for the simple crime of being born. However, Cordy turns out to be a person who embraces change and is able to learn and grow, both from the positive influences in her life and the massive curveballs she's thrown.

When Cordelia falls for the charms of one Xander Harris, she initially insists on keeping their romance secret due to the inequality of their social status. It actually isn't long before she realizes that not only does she not want to keep their love secret but actually that it isn't in her nature – she's no "sheep," like Harmony. She's proud of their relationship even if no-one else cool approves, and that's a lesson for all of us. What's more, when Xander cheats on Cordelia, she doesn't accept his groveling. He threw away their love, so it's his loss. Get gone, loser!

When her family loses all their money due to her father's tax fraud, does she bitch and moan? Hell no, she gets a job, saves for the killer prom dress and accepts her college dreams are over (even though, FYI, she got into all the best party schools, Xander).

Once she teams up with Angel in LA, things go into overdrive. Accepting her painful visions as a necessary evil shows us all that sometimes it's worth suffering for the greater good. This is typified by her final, dying act of gifting Angel with one last vision and allowing him to save millions. Not bad for the bougie bitch driving Daddy's car in high school.

Best Traits
Filled with self-belief, direct and honest, steely in her determination, killer fashion sense.

"
Tact is just not saying true stuff. I'll pass.
"

Life Lesson

BEING OPEN EXPERIENCES TO NEW

As graduation stunts go, blowing up your high school and the Mayor is a pretty dramatic one which, it goes without saying, is not to be attempted yourself. You can find those instructions in *Be More Evil*. This is not that book.

Heading off to college, therefore, was pretty nerve-wracking for Ms. Summers. Her boyfriend had left her, Willow was seriously into Oz, and Xander had last been seen heading off, *On the Road*–style, in his car. School had been literal Hell for Buffy, so moving somewhere new was fraught with anxiety and generally gave her the wiggins.

In true Buffy style she did have to deal with a demonic roommate (literally), a monster-hunting government agency under a frat house and the return of Spike, but she grew to love college. New teachers saw her excel academically, she made a stack of new friends, and met a certain farm-bred Iowan called Riley Finn. Getting to this point, though, required a huge dollop of courage and self-belief, as even our heroine had to battle homesickness and anxiety on the way.

The takeaway

Buffy beat it and so can you!

1. **Find ways to meet new people:** It might feel terrifying, but join any group you can. Whether it's your office gym class, a local wine society, a gaming team … or even your local coven, meeting with like-minded people will only help your life feel richer.

2. **People are, generally, nice:** When we're feeling nervous we often think that people might see the faults we do. In reality, most people are kind and decent and just want others to like them too.

3. **Go at your own speed:** There is no set time about how long it takes someone to adjust to somewhere new. Whatever pace you're comfortable with, is the right one.

Be more
Oz!

Fact: Werewolves make lousy boyfriends. The constant destruction of the clothes you've bought them to replace the hideous ones they were wearing when you met, is probably just one of the many issues. Trying to eat you once a month is a biggie too!

That said, Oz is a pretty awesome boyfriend to Willow – kind, calm and supportive and sensible enough to lock himself up when the full moon comes. All is going stellar until he decides to leave Sunnydale, and Willow, to tame his raging inner beast. From Willow's POV this is a big betrayal but in hindsight stopping yourself from ripping random strangers to shreds is probably a key part of #livingyourbestlife.

Oz gives up the woman he loves to master his inner demons, he recognizes the sickness inside himself and goes out to fix it. Many of us are plagued by inner demons too. Often it's essential we work through them with our loved ones, but sometimes the right thing to do is take a step back, spend the time healing and getting ourselves on the right path again.

This can be heartbreaking to those we love, and ourselves, but sometimes the greatest act of love can be walking away. So be kind and loving to your partner like Oz but also, if things get too much, have the strength to do the right thing too, even if it's tough.

Best Traits
Quiet, humble, strong, noble, philosophical.

"I'm going through some ... changes."

51

LOSING A LOVED ONE

Buffy's mom, Joyce Summers, was a remarkable woman. Being forced to relocate to a different town and start a new life in her forties was a tough gig. Throw in a teenage daughter who also happened to be responsible for saving the world 24/7 and you have a situation that would have driven even the strongest woman crazy. Not only did she make it through the rough years of Buffy's adolescence, with all the madness that Angel, Spike and her own robot boyfriend Ted created, she continued to be gentle, kind, accepting and loving.

Joyce being diagnosed with brain cancer was hard to see as it reminds us we can't guarantee that we, or our loved ones, won't get sick. All we can do is face such situations with courage, fortitude and a dose of humor. When Joyce was recovering from surgery, she still had time to make a joke with her two beloved daughters.

The heart breaking moment when Buffy comes home to find her mom passed away on the sofa from a hemorrhage, is a moment just as terrifying and upsetting as any of the epic battles that Buffy faced. This was the one fight that Buffy didn't and couldn't win as, ironically, the one thing her superhuman powers couldn't defeat was the most human of foes, illness.

The takeaway

When sickness or death happens, things move out of our control. We can only try to not only be more Buffy, but also be more Dawn, Willow, Xander and the others, whose support got the Summers girls through the darkest hours.

What we *can* control is how much love and support we give to those who need it if they experience sickness or loss – whether it's cleaning their house, doing their shopping or just being there to talk to. Don't assume that people want to be alone with their grief. Sometimes we are tested in ways that are deeply unfair. We'll win some fights, others we'll lose. But the important thing is to never give up and never feel like you're alone.

Life Lesson

BEING AN ALLY

Back in the pre-woke days of the late 90s, most of the world was still yoked under laws and social conventions that made being gay a tough existence – everywhere was like living on the Hellmouth if you weren't straight. Thankfully, people are now more able to freely and confidently express their sexual identity, which is a beautiful sight to behold – #loveislove.

Willow falling in love with Tara was a big moment for a lot of young gay people, who got to see a loving, gay relationship broadcast into their homes. Seeing Willow go on a journey of self-discovery, watching her fall in love, and seeing the joy and confidence that love brought out in Tara, was a powerful piece of magic.

Unusually for the times, but not unsurprisingly, the Scoobies adjusted to Willow's coming out with barely more than a comment. Perhaps it was seeing the change in happiness that Tara brought, or maybe it was just relief that Willow's new plus-one was less likely to eat them than her previous partner, werewolf Oz.

But being an ally remains as important as ever. With the awakening of people's minds to myriad different orientations and gender identities, there has been an equal and opposite reaction against it – Newton's Third Law of Assholes maybe? Even those of us in the LGBTQ+ family need to stick up for our fellow members.

The takeaway

1. **Be active:** Go on that march, sign that petition, slay that charity ball! Do whatever you can to raise awareness of social issues. If you don't, who will?

2. **Educate yourself:** The world is moving fast – like wicked fast. We're becoming more aware of new identities and ways of living by the year. Make sure you understand the community who you're speaking for.

3. **Enjoy it:** Being an ally is a great gift – for the world, other people and your soul. While passion is crucial, try and remember that the freedom to feel joy and love is what you're fighting for.

Be more Tara !

Some people are born with so much confidence that it's practically high-kicking out of every pore. There's another tribe of humanity, though, who don't hog the limelight, living in a world where museums and old bookstores are their natural home. These people are very like the much loved and much missed Tara, the quiet witch and Willow's great love.

Best Traits
Compassionate, understanding, caring, forgiving, puts people before herself.

Tara was criminally shy when we met her, a wallflower barely capable of speaking a word in front of others and always seemingly apologising for her existence. However, with time, and encouragement, she blossomed, overcoming her shyness to reveal a passionate, strong woman.

Tara's journey to self-love and acceptance wasn't easy, but it is one we can be inspired by:

✱ Grow and nurture your self-confidence as everyone, EVERYONE has something to offer this world. Don't let anybody make you feel otherwise. Willow helped Tara find her confidence and purpose, so look for people in your life who will help you find yours.

✱ Tara escaped from her controlling and manipulative relatives and found her real fam in the Scoobies. Sometimes the family we find and choose are our real family, not those we are born with.

When I feel like there's no way out, when I'm at my worst ... you always make me feel so special. How do you do that?

SURVIVING THE DAILY GRIND

Super strength, preternatural speed, reflexes that would make a ninja green – all gifts for being the Chosen One. What it doesn't come with is a salary, which is particularly galling, since few other jobs are as inherently dangerous as being humanity's sole defender against the Forces of Evil.

As such, after her mom died, Buffy was forced to get a job. And, despite being educated, personable, snatched and ... well ... lethal, the only job she could find was at the Doublemeat Palace – a burger joint as grim as it sounds. Buffy wasn't thrilled and, after she had resolved the issue of a leech demon hiding in an old woman's head (and frankly who hasn't had one of those?), she settles down and gets on with it.

The takeaway

Sometimes in life we have to do things to make rent. Sometimes our jobs are our passions and we feel blessed – but not that often. Most of us will, at some point in our lives, have to grind through a job that is just tolerable, which kinda sucks. However Buffy shows us that the best approach to a shitty job is:

1. **Suck it up:** There are people in some parts of the world literally dying to get work. You can cope with creepy Kenneth in IT and a persistent lack of teaspons in the office kitchen.

2. **Be proud:** No matter what you do, be proud of it. There's nothing wrong with any job. High-five to you for making your own way in this world!

3. **Do your best:** A bad attitude will not only make you miserable, but also infect everyone else. Be a radiator not a drain.

"MAKE YOUR CHOICE. ARE YOU READY

"

TOXIC RELATIONSHIPS

We've all made some bad choices in love. It's part of being human. Falling in love with Angel wasn't something that Buffy intended and, while it had its lows (the understatement of the millennia), it did give Buffy the happy.

Spike, on the other hand, was an affair that Buffy came to regret. In a short space of time she had gained a sister, lost her mother, died, got resurrected and then lost Giles – a period with more turbulence than a drone flying through a tornado. She sought solace in the arms of someone who ignited the passion that was missing from her life, while using her dislike of him to maintain emotional distance. The fact that Spike was seriously hot was just an added bonus.

The takeaway

We've all been there – been involved with someone who doesn't treat us well or, if we're being 100 percent honest here, we don't treat well. Not every relationship is The One and that's OK. But if we find ourselves in a relationship like Buffy and Spike's, where we're compromising our values and feeling ashamed, maybe we should think about a few things:

1. **Everyone has feelings:** Even if you don't think the relationship is significant, bear in mind that the other party might, so go easy.

2. **Stand in their shoes:** It can be useful sometimes to imagine how the other person feels in a certain situation. When things are a bit fractious we tend to think only our perspective is correct.

3. **Don't be afraid to walk away:** Sometimes it's better to be alone, than to be with someone but be unhappy. If a relationship isn't working, be like Buffy and have the courage to leave. You can feel more lonely in a bad relationship.

Buffy and Spike didn't last because there was no foundation to build anything on. Eventually Buffy found the courage to admit her feelings to Spike, and also to walk away. Bravery takes many forms and the courage to leave a toxic relationship is huge. Be strong.

Be more
Anya!

Anya has one of the best and most ridiculous backstories of anyone in the Buffyverse – a 1000-year-old ex-vengeance demon, obsessed with money and terrified of rabbits. Her love for Xander is simultaneously heart warming and slightly bizarre – and how many fucks did she give about other people's opinions? ZERO!

This is what is so awesome about Anya. Even the Scoobies thought she was wacky for having the hots for Xander, but did she care? Nope! Was she embarrassed about loving money (to the point she wanted to trade her children in while playing The Game of Life)? Hell to the no!

Feisty as a sack of weasels and as sassy as a sugared-up nine-year-old, Anya was unique. As if this wasn't enough, like the rest of the gang, she was brave, and also knowledgeable in a way that only someone who can personally remember the year 1492 could be.

Best Traits
Unashamed to be who she wants to be or say what she wants to say, sweet yet ferociously unique, wicked sense of humor.

She protected her friends and ultimately gave her life to save fellow Scooby and vampire, Andrew. After a millennium of visiting vengeance on men, she meets her maker by saving one – maybe one that didn't deserve it – but she wasn't judge, jury and executioner anymore, just a kind, brave woman doing what was right.

> "I promise to love you, to cherish you, to honor you, uh, not to obey you, of course, because that's anachronistic and misogynistic and who do you think you are, like a sea captain or something?"

What would Buffy do?
NEVERTHELESS, SHE PERSISTED.
Challenging Authority

Buffy was forever being told what she could or couldn't do by a series of men, some of them deeply evil like the Mayor or Adam but, others, like the Watchers Council, were meant to be on her side. Everywhere she turned there was always a man telling her what she could or couldn't do. She ultimately killed most of them, which is a pretty effective tactic tbh, but not one you should try and recreate – unless you fancy being told what to do by a prison warder for the rest of your life!

So maybe your boss is telling you that you can't have that promotion. Or your teacher never asks your opinion in class. Perhaps someone in your soccer team always talks over you when you want to talk tactics? In these cases you need to think WWBD?:

Fight with words not fists: While Buffy would ultimately dispatch her evil enemies with violence, when she came up against sexism or prejudice she always fought back verbally. Indulging your baser instincts is tempting, but ultimately there are some battles that need to be fought with words.

Never let it get you down: It can be really hard to have to listen to negativity and criticism from haters and, after a while, it can seep into you. Don't let it! It's hard to keep your strength up day after day, but if you start to believe it for a single second, stop!

Challenge sexism: Don't be sucked into the limiting ideas of what men and women are and can be.

SELF-CARE, SLAYER STYLE

Buffy and the Scoobies had a tough time! Battling the forces of evil is Hell on your nerves and your nails. Be more like Buffy and the gang and do the following:

1. **When in doubt, sweat it out:** There was not a problem for Buffy that couldn't be helped by attacking some punching pads in the gym. Keep yourself in good shape by doing something that raises your heart rate every day. Plus you'll know you have a heart that's still beating. Win!

2. **In the cookie of life, friends are the chocolate chips:** Nothing wasn't made better in the Buffyverse by sharing it with one of the Scoobies (unless it was Spike – don't share anything with Spike!). Share often and deeply with your friends. Even literal Hell can be made better with a buddy by your side.

3. **All work and no play makes Buffy a dull girl:** Yes life can be serious but, unless you're Buffy, you only get one, so make sure you enjoy it! We work to live, not live to work. Party, dance, laugh and revel in a world that hasn't gone to Hell ... yet.

Affirmations

Never feel you are powerless, even if you don't have superhuman qualities. Read these affirmations out loud, record them on your phone or sing them in the shower!

1. The only thing that can stop me, is me.

2. Slayers don't quit.

3. I have been chosen to save my own world.

What would Buffy do?

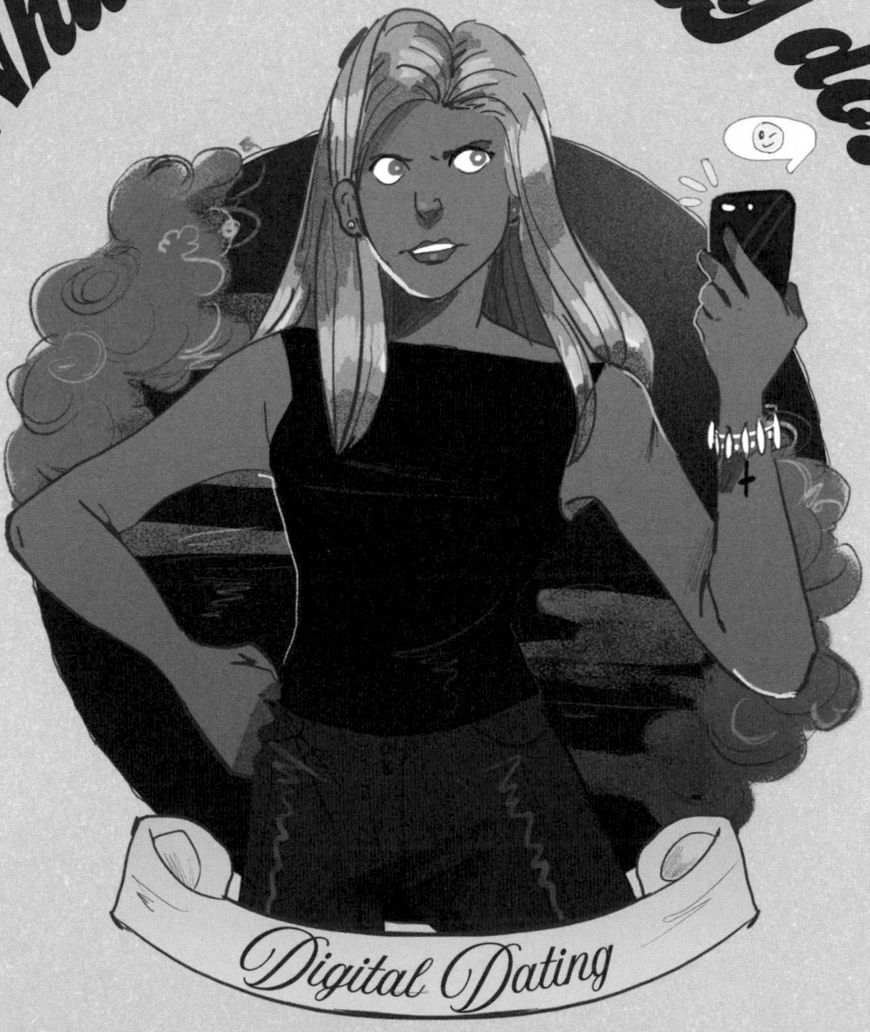

It seems crazy now to think that Buffy existed in a world where you were more likely to come across a runaway teenage demon with a Cher fixation than you were a smartphone. Demon slayage would be a lot easier with access to Google Maps, Wikipedia and WhatsApp groups to coordinate the Scoobies' movements.

What the Buffster would have been grateful for is the lack of Tinder, Bumble and other dating apps in her life. Her taste in men ranged from the puppy-faced but deeply insecure Riley to the frankly murderous Spike, so not being able to swipe right on a range of soulless immortals would have been a win for Team Buffy!

But for many of us, "The Swipes" are our main path to dates, love and occasional lust. We live in a world in which we look at hordes of potential partners before our first pumpkin spice latte of the day, have three Tinder dates a week and spend our lunchbreaks alternating between being furious and devastated about being ghosted by real estate agents called Tim or Tiffany.

But what would Buffy have done in the warzone that is dating today? Any and all of the following probably:

- ✝ Not take shit from anyone who is two-timing her: If you want the Chosen One you get to choose only one, I'm afraid.

- ✝ Treat everybody she meets with kindness and respect: Buffy understands more than most that what you see on the surface isn't always the same as what lies beneath.

- ✝ Give people the benefit of the doubt once, but any subsequent crappy dating behavior won't be tolerated: Buffy didn't save the world repeatedly AND die twice to be sent unsolicited dick pics without saying anything.

They say dating is Hell. And what did Buffy do to the Hellmouth? Kick. Its. Ass!

Be more

Angel!

Tall. Dark. Handsome. Dead. Mmm, Angel possessed all the qualities you would want in a man. He fell in love with Buffy from the moment he saw her and, with the exception of a brief interlude when he became psychotically evil, his feelings for her never changed.

Transformed by vampire blood from a drunken layabout to an A-grade hottie who could brood professionally, Angel went on a journey of self-discovery like no other. Once his soul had been restored, he embarked on a quest of repentance, trying to wash his hands clean after a century of bloody mayhem. Angel learned that when you make mistakes, hiding from the world is not the solution. To atone you need to face up to them, which is *the* lesson we can learn from him.

Face up to them he did, becoming a powerful warrior for good and saving countless lives. Sadly, however, like many great love stories, his and Buffy's time together was doomed. It broke her heart but he knew that as an ageless dead creature he needed to leave to truly let Buffy live. A heartbreaking choice but one that required unbelievable strength and courage.

Best Traits
Noble, brave, a deep understanding of the power of sacrifice, the archetypal dark hero.

"All that matters
is what we do.
'Cause that's
all there is.
What we do."

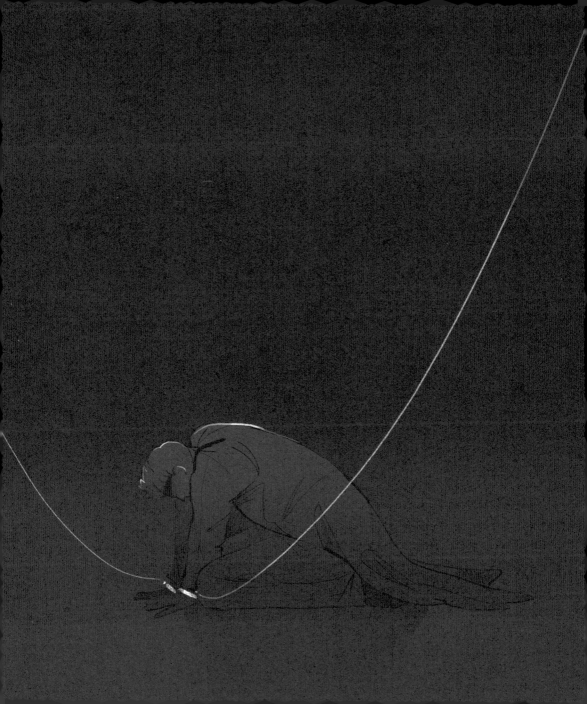

Life Lesson

FORGiVENESS

Buffy plunging a sword through Angel's heart and sending him to Hell is one of the jaw-on-the-floor moments of Buffy. While it was needed to save the world from being sucked into the underworld, it still shocked us to see Buffy kill the man she loved. We were even more shook when he emerged a few months later (nude – swoon!) but not nearly as freaked out as the Scoobies were when Buffy brought him back into their lives again.

Buffy saw something in Angel, though, that was genuinely repentant and that he wanted to make amends. His behavior forever altered his relationships with the gang but he fought his way back into their hearts.

The key point here is that Angel took responsibility for his actions and made amends to those he had hurt – key steps for any of us who transgress. What he also did was give people time. Forgiveness doesn't come easy but it can be earned.

It's not only Angel who's saved by being given a second chance. Faith and Spike are too. Remember that the next time someone in your life messes up. Forgiveness can be a powerful gift.

"To forgive is an act of compassion, Buffy. It's … it's … it's not done because people deserve it. It's done because they need it."
– Giles

Life Lesson

TRUSTING JUDGMENT

YOUR OWN

If there was to be a more British stereotype than Wesley Wyndham-Pryce it would have to be Queen Elizabeth II riding a giant corgi through Buckingham Palace singing Adele. He was *ludicrously* British. While not exactly a bad person, he was a classic example of someone placed into authority by virtue of who he was, not his abilities.

Buffy, being the good ol' team player that she was, went along with this for a while but eventually came to an important realization. She was listening to the judgment of someone else, when she should have been listening to her own – and she was the damn Slayer! Wesley probably felt he had her best interests at heart but, in reality, he was following his own agenda and using Buffy.

Now, advice is important, and Giles was a literal life-saver on many an occasion, but importantly he helped Buffy live a better life. However, Wesley wanted to choose the path that life went. If you find yourself in a situation where someone is directing you down a certain path that you're not sure about, ask yourself: Is this where I want to go? If the answer is no, you know what to do!

The takeaway

Self-belief isn't the easiest tap to turn on but, remember, the person who is most likely to be the best expert in you is ... drum roll please ... you!

Be more Spike!

Before Spike was Spike, he was William the Bloody – seemingly a fearsome nickname until we realize its origin lies in his "bloody awful" poetry as a mortal. And "Spike?" Well that came from his penchant for torturing people with a railroad spike – or some say that it's because they'd rather have a spike through their head than listen to his poetry. To be honest, Spike seems like a pretty crap role model, alive or dead – at first.

In the early days, Spike was just the latest villain, and his overwhelming desire was to kill Buffy any which way he could. Not exemplary stuff. As we wandered through the years though and he spent more time in the Buffyverse, he starts to grow and deepen.

First he's neutered by technology, then by his love for Buffy, and finally he too has his soul returned. As these events overtake him we (and he!) discover that despite the raging demon inside him, a sliver of humanity remains dormant, waiting to be reanimated.

His final act is to willingly sacrifice himself to destroy the Hellmouth, an act of bravery that marks his redemption. So yes he's committed terrible crimes, yes he has awful taste in soap operas, but he keeps trying to be a better man. We have to ask ourselves what is worse – an evil person who knows it and tries to do good? Or a good person who doesn't realize they're doing evil?

Best Traits
A fearless devotion to those he loves, self-sacrificing, passionate, romantic.

> **I have come to redefine the words pain and suffering since I fell in love with you.**

Life Lesson

ACCEPTANCE of OTHERS

Little sisters are supposed to be annoying, it's their purpose in life! So it's fair to say Dawn NAILS this role. From the first minute we see her she's already winding Buffy up – taking her stuff without asking, eavesdropping and constantly almost being killed. A veritable holy trinity of ASB (Annoying Sister Behavior).

While a sister magically appearing from nowhere was a pretty WTF moment for us, Dawn finding out she was in fact a mystical ball of energy was pretty WTF for her too. Buffy, being the total trooper she is, takes this all in her stride. She accepts Dawn into her family, along with her mom, and ultimately gives her life to protect Dawn from Glory, a god from a Hell dimension.

The takeaway

Acceptance is something we all crave, and finding your home in this world is a feeling like no other. When we look at the people in our lives, we probably see the things we love about them but also their flaws, whether it's our co-workers or members of our family. Everyone has both.

So let's bear the following in mind:

1. **Even the most saintly among us has flaws:** If we always look for flaws, we'll always find them and always be disappointed.

2. **Accept people for who they are, not who we want them to be:** This is the path to happy and healthy relationships.

3. **Acceptance is a two-way gift:** The more understanding and kind about others you are, the more likely you'll treat yourself, and be treated, the same way.

Be more Dawn!

Poor Dawn. Many people have, shall we say … "strong" feelings about Buffy's little sister.

Two main factors seem to be at play here:

1. She's incredibly annoying.

2. She doesn't exist until Buffy goes to college.

The thing is, younger siblings are supposed to be annoying. TBF to Dawn, though, she does have a tough time – even Freud would struggle with unpicking the psychological gordian knot that is being both a 13-year-old girl AND a mystical ball of energy that could potentially destroy the multiverse.

Once the crisis with Glory is over, though, and after the death of her sister Buffy, Dawn rises. The annoying shrill teenager is replaced by a mature young woman who, much like Buffy, takes on a huge responsibility at a young age. Ironically, bearing in mind her origin, she has no superpower. Like Xander she is just an ordinary human doing extraordinary things. Right before the climactic battle Xander acknowledges this beautifully:

"They'll never know how tough it is, Dawnie, to be the one who isn't chosen. To live so near to the spotlight and never step in it. But I know. I see more than anybody realizes because nobody's watching me. I saw you last night. I see you working here today. You're not special. You're extraordinary."

Best Traits
Grace and humility – the ability to always be the backup and never the star, courageous.

> **"You've made these amazing sacrifices – for me ... for the world. I've always wondered if I could do something like that. If I could be that brave. It's kinda cool to find out that I can. I'll do it. I want to do it."**

"There is only one thing on this earth more powerful than evil, and that's us."

THE POWER OF SACRIFICE

"Death is your gift."

When these words are whispered to Buffy she interprets them as telling her that she is the bringer of death. Bet she was thrilled. It's only when the battle with Glory is almost lost that she realizes the true meaning of them – giving her own life to save her sister's is the greatest gift she can give.

Since most of us aren't vampire slayers we aren't required to give our lives to save our loved ones – phew. But the lesson that Buffy teaches us about sacrifice is important, as sacrifice is both powerful and complex. Putting others before yourself and serving their needs at the expense of your own is selfless and noble ... to a point.

The takeaway

Thinking "Do I really need this more than you?" or, "Will you value this more than I do?" will probably lead you to actions that are good for the soul – altruism, kindness and generosity.

But crucially, too much sacrifice can be bad, stripping away the things you need until you are left with nothing. This is not noble, it's kinda ... dumb. The power from giving something up comes from when you make a decision about who genuinely needs something more. When it becomes your default at the expense of yourself, it's actually a form of self-harm.

So give the gift when it's right. It could change someone's life, but don't do it unless you really understand its power.

DUSTING YOURSELF OFF

No-one would argue that Buffy didn't have a tough time of it. She was someone who three unbelievable things would happen to before breakfast. Whether it was being pulled into a prison work camp in a Hell dimension, almost being burned at the stake by her mother, or having to dig herself out of her own grave, Buffy graduated magna cum laude from the school of hard knocks.

True, she was supernaturally enhanced, but Buffy never let life crush her. Even when the latest Big Bad was threatening to destroy her, or one of her boyfriends was firmly exiting stage left, she still got up every day, dusted herself off and walked out that front door again.

The takeaway

Some people don't think they naturally have resilence, and that it's a trait like blue eyes or webbed toes. The strength to go on is in all of us. It might be buried deep inside but it is there. And once you find it, it can make you stronger than you were before. So when the shit hits the Hellmouth, don't give up. Look inside yourself and find the ember of fortitude. Find it and stoke it into a bonfire!

"Even if you see them coming, you're not ready for the big moments. No-one asks for their life to change, not really. But it does, so what are we? Helpless? Puppets? Nah. The big moments are gonna come, you can't help that. It's what you do afterwards that counts. That's when you find out who you are." – Whistler

THiNK BiG, BE BOLD

Legend has it that the Slayers were created by a group of men who harnessed the power of an ancient being, forced it into a woman's body and thus the line of Slayers was born. There is a certain perversity in having enough power to fuse a human into a demon but only enough to make one.

Poetic? Yes. Practical? No.

Anyway, faced with the End of the World (v. 363) Buffy and Willow hatch an audacious plan to turn every potential slayer into an actual one, thereby changing the balance in the battle of Good vs. Evil forever. Aside from being a generally badass plan, what's amazing about this approach is that it takes the status quo, pops it into a paper bag and smashes it with a hammer.

The takeaway

There's something really inspiring here about a group of people faced with an impossible sitch who respond with an impossible-sounding solution. In our daily lives we hopefully won't come across many situations that feel impossible to solve but, if we do and it all feels a little hopeless, then maybe the best solution is to think big.

Audacious thinking can be frightening and takes a huge amount of self-belief, but it's worth the investment if you do it right. Try to visualiz1e what you want to achieve and imagine for a moment that there are no limits. Think big, think positive and focus on the overall picture. It could change your life!

ONCE MORE, WITH FEELING

Buffy changed lives – both in the show and in real life. Even the simplest Google search will reveal the legions of fans who were impacted by the perky Ms. Summers. For some it was just a fun TV show, for others it demonstrated that being shy, geeky or unpopular at high school didn't mean that you couldn't amount to something.

It broke boundaries in showing one of the first long-term gay relationships in a TV show, and tackled some pretty tough subjects, especially those that many of us will face in this life. The show was as brave as the Buffster herself.

A lifetime of lessons are wrapped up in those 144 episodes alone and hopefully everyone can take something important away from the show. Maybe it's how to be brave in the face of a terrifying or emotionally challenging situation, forgiving people for their mistakes, or learning to have faith in your own abilities. The importance of finding good friends is one of the strongest messages.

Chuck on an episode every now and again or do the full seven-season binge – you'll always learn something new.

We're always told to never meet our heroes as they will ultimately disappoint us. It just goes to show that conventional wisdom is bullshit as we met Buffy every week for seven happy years. She may have sometimes messed up but she never let us down.

Legend. Hero. Role Model. Be More Buffy!

" No weapons.

No friends.

No hope.

Take all that away and what's left? "

"ME."

Smith Street Books

Published in 2020 by Smith Street Books
Naarm | Melbourne | Australia
smithstreetbooks.com

ISBN: 978-1-92581-150-6

Publisher: Paul McNally
Project editor: Hannah Koelmeyer
Editor: Ariana Klepac
Design and layout: Alissa Dinallo
Illustrations: YoungEarlGrey, IllustrationX
Proofreader: Pam Dunne

Printed & bound in China by C&C Offset Printing Co., Ltd.

Book 127
10 9 8 7 6 5 4 3 2 1